D0961645

How to Survive a
GARDEN GNOME ATTACK

How to Survive a
GARDEN GNOME ATTACK

Defend Yourself
When the Lawn Warriors Strike
(and They Will)

CHUCK SAMBUCHINO

Photography by Andrew Parsons

TEN SPEED PRESS
Berkeley

This guide is dedicated to Janosh "The Gnome Hunter" Onderdonk, Captain Bjorn Presthus, Millie Palmer, and the 126 souls on board National Airways Flight 4663. All were brave individuals whose lives were cut short. Rest in peace, freedom fighters.

Copyright © 2010 by Chuck Sambuchino
Photography © 2010 by Andrew Parsons
Photograph on page 14 © 2010 by Sara Guren
Left photograph on page 97 ©iStockphoto.com/fpm
Right photograph on page 97 ©iStockphoto.com/logoHY
Left photograph on page 98 ©iStockphoto.com/MogensTrolle
Right photograph on page 98 ©iStockphoto.com/Pgiam
Left photograph on page 99 ©iStockphoto.com/-M-I-S-H-A-
Right photograph on page 99 ©iStockphoto.com/apz01

Published in the United States by Ten Speed Press, an imprint of
the Crown Publishing Group, a division of Random House, Inc., New York.
www.crownpublishing.com
www.tenspeed.com

Ten Speed Press and the Ten Speed Press colophon are registered trademarks of
Random House, Inc.

Library of Congress Cataloging-in-Publication Data

Sambuchino, Chuck.
  How to survive a garden gnome attack : defend yourself when the lawn warriors
strike (and they will) / Chuck Sambuchino. — 1st ed.
      p. cm.
  1. American wit and humor. I. Title.
  PN6165.S26 2010
  818'.602—dc22

                              2010008806

ISBN 978-1-58008-463-5

Printed in Singapore

Cover and interior design by Betsy Stromberg
Cover photography by Betsy Stromberg

10 9 8 7 6 5 4 3 2 1

First Edition

CONTENTS

INTRODUCTION

Keep reading if you want to live.

Call them what you want. Garden gnomes. Lawn ornaments. Little evil outdoor statuary hell-bent on world domination. It doesn't matter. What does matter is that, right now, they're hiding in plain sight, pretending to be symbols of merriment and good will. But secretly, quietly, while pushing diminutive wheelbarrows and brandishing miniature flowerpots, they're planning home invasions all over the world. Perhaps they're in your backyard right now—and you're staring at one while reading this. (Wait a minute—does that gnome look a little closer to the patio door than yesterday?)

Fear not. Now that you know they're planning to strike, you're much safer than you were sixty seconds ago. The next thing to do is learn everything you can about how to protect yourself, your loved ones, and your residence from these malicious garden dwellers. Do you know how to stop a gnome from tunneling under the house? What is the best (really the only) way to combat several gnomes at once in close quarters? How to interpret their communication? Would you recognize the signs of a gathering hoard or an impending infiltration? If you answered no to any of these questions, it's a good thing you're reading this handbook.

How to Survive a Garden Gnome Attack is the only survival guide that instructs you on how to prevent and ward off a home invasion and eradicate them from your property for good. In the unfortunate event of an actual attack, it will prepare you for battle, outlining dozens of possible encounter scenarios and defense strategies. It is important to read the book in its entirety for a thorough understanding of what you and millions like you are dealing with. And after you've finished reading, you'll be ready to face the pointy-capped little men waiting outside and save your own life in the process.

If you think you have time to waste, rest assured you do not. Right this very minute, garden gnomes are conspiring and mobilizing in your neighborhood. This problem is not going to go away—and never forget that gnomes cannot be domesticated. This is war. They want you dead, and they may succeed—unless you're ready. And if you think it could never happen to you because of who you are or where you live or what you look like, trust me when I tell you that they have you in their sights. It doesn't matter where you were born or whether you're sixteen or eighty. These wily warriors are out to exterminate humanity, one gnomeowner at a time.

So before you continue, take a moment to make sure all your doors and windows are secured—that includes pet doors. Background or white noise in the room (a small fan works well) is advisable to disrupt any possible enchantments. Do that and then come back. We'll wait. They won't.

ASSESS

1

ARE YOU AT RISK?

If you're reading this book, chances are you're in proximity to garden gnomes (*Gnomus hortus*) and have made the most important decision of your life: to educate yourself and take a stand against these suburban subversives. As gnomes continue to populate the planet at an alarming rate, we are all at risk—some more than others. Some of us will have years to wait before we have to fight a lawn gnome to the death in single combat. Scarily, some of us have days at most before forces clash. Your first step should be to assess the probability level of an attack on your domicile:

Factors *increasing* your risk of an attack:

▲ For some insane reason, you actually own lawn gnomes.
▲ You live in a suburban or rural house.

- ▲ Your dwelling sits on secluded, wooded acreage.
- ▲ You live alone.
- ▲ You follow a strict routine, making it easy to predict your comings and goings.
- ▲ There are gnomeowners in your neighborhood.

Factors *decreasing* your risk of an attack:

- ▲ You've never seen a garden gnome except in pictures or on TV.
- ▲ You live in an urban area with little green space.
- ▲ You live in an apartment complex or high-rise.
- ▲ You travel frequently.
- ▲ You frequently move among your many residences because you're rich.
- ▲ You live with a large, extended family, whose members all watch over one another.

If you possess three or more factors that increase the likelihood of a lawn ornament onslaught, you are no doubt a "high-risk" target. Stop everything you're doing and carve out an afternoon to finish reading this book. (Even slow-witted readers can manage this—it's only 106 pages.) When you're done, go out and buy supplies to protect yourself—then come back, start fortifying your home, and read this guide again.

Are You at Risk?

2

Suspicious Activity

According to garden gnome defense expert David Lamay, every household assault is preceded by deep reconnaissance and probing (DRAP). Such scrutiny increases a gnome's chances of success as well as the chances of your burial. Similar to thieves casing a store before a robbery, gnomes will try and find out as much as they can about you, your home, and your habits before mounting an offensive. Prior to a strike, gnomes perform months or even years of reconnaissance work—scoping out every detail of your day-to-day routine and any vulnerabilities in your residential defenses. This pre-attack investigation is called probing, and a conscious gnomeowner will begin to notice unusual and disturbing signs in and around the house, garden, and outbuildings (detached garage, garden shed, pool house, etc.).

Start to think about probing in terms of *location*. When they enter and explore your territory—the house—they're probing *you*. But at the same time, you can probe them right back. The backyard is their territory. When you're outside, take the initiative and start assessing *them*. A note of caution: Although you're fairly safe in open spaces, it is never recommended to follow a gnome into the woods should you see one leave the lawn and head for the trees. Consider this to be crossing the Gnome Rubicon; you're on their turf—in their world. If you step out of the familiarity of your backyard and into the black hole that is the forest, your chances of survival decrease by 60 percent, while your odds of getting bludgeoned to death at the thicket's edge increase by 200,000 percent.

So why haven't you been attacked yet? That's a good question—a question by someone who wants to stay alive. The answer is they're still evaluating the situation and weighing the pros and cons of an attack. Perhaps you already have solid home defenses in place and didn't realize it. Perhaps the gnomes decided to assault your neighbors first. Or perhaps your life is on the agenda for tomorrow.

Sightings and Strange Phenomena

Things to watch for outside the house include the following:

▲ **Footprints in dirt or mud:** Gnomes will try to cover their tracks with trickery, but sometimes they will let their guard down. If you see small shoeprints in wet earth, you know a gnome has been prowling.

▲ **Misplaced wheelbarrow:** If they're moving tools or stones, they'll need to use a wheelbarrow. Look for indentations in the grass and watch for wheelbarrows where they shouldn't be (right outside the front door or in the middle of the driveway). Give your wheelbarrow a quick hose blast. If you find residue on your next inspection, that's a clue that danger is afoot.

▲ **Unexplained movement:** You're weeding a flower bed or cutting the grass when you suddenly stop and just stare at a lawn gnome. Your pulse quickens because something isn't . . . quite . . . right. (Was the gnome in the red cap sitting *to the right* of the birdbath yesterday? Was the gnome in the blue tunic always *on the bottom step* of the stairs to the deck?) What you're feeling is a combination of adrenaline and intuition. Pay attention.

▲ **Sensation of being watched:** Psychiatrists will say that we cannot actually "feel" eyes boring into the back of our heads, but they also insist that lawn gnomes pose no threat to humanity whatsoever—proving they obviously know nothing.

▲ **Homegrown produce stunted/discolored:** First of all, stop eating from your garden—immediately. It's too easy for a gnome to taint your homegrown tomatoes and strawberries, and keep in mind that most gnome potions won't wash off with a quick rinse under the kitchen tap. Look for unusual size and coloring, disturbing outgrowths, or premature rotting.

▲ **Inexplicable animal behavior:** You're not looking for specific behaviors, but rather for baffling deviations

from the norm. Are birds no longer coming to the feeder? Are local nocturnal mammals (raccoons, possums) venturing out in daylight? Is your dog barking "at nothing" or urinating on himself? All of these are telltale signs of looming doom.

Possibly worse than suspecting strange goings on are afoot outside your house is noticing alarming occurrences happening *inside* your dwelling. Things to watch out for indoors include the following:

▲ **Pipe smoke:** Gnomes should know better than to smoke inside a house, but a rare, undisciplined warrior may light up and give you a precious clue that intruders have breached the perimeter.

▲ **Sawdust:** Wood shavings indicate they've entered through a baseboard, kitchen cupboard, or bathroom vanity, or they're tunneling up through the floor or down through a ceiling beam. It's time to start checking attics, basements, and crawlspaces for gnome passageways.

▲ **Toolbox missing/emptied:** Your toolbox is the Holy Grail to a gnome. Think about it. The average toolbox contains devices perfectly designed for stabbing and puncturing (screwdrivers, drills), bludgeoning (hammers, wrenches), dismembering (pliers, hand-saws), and crushing (mallets, crowbars). Toolboxes are rarely removed altogether because of their weight and location (on a shelf or workbench in the garage), but if it does turn up missing—or is significantly lighter—it's not the annoying neighbor's kid. . . .

▲ **Cameras/video camcorders missing/manipulated:** A gnome's greatest allies are human ignorance and disbelief. Either we don't know they're a threat, or we just can't *believe* they're a threat. If only we could catch them moving on camera, we could educate the world. Gnomes understand the potential danger, so one of their first acts of probing will be to find and disable any recording devices you have—including video apps on your cell phone—so that, whatever happens, you have no "proof of life" apart from your injuries.

▲ **Utensils/appliances missing/moved:** Have you ever opened your utensil or cutlery drawer and wondered where all the knives went? Well, now you know. Silverware will be among the first things gnomes nab. In addition, any small appliance with a detachable blade (vegetable peeler, coffee grinder, blender, food processor) must be kept under lock and key. Other household items to keep a close watch on include nail files, ballpoint pens, and scissors (all sizes).

▲ **House drafts:** You can't understand it. You keep inching up the thermostat yet the house remains chilly. What's wrong? Then you start to notice some parts of the house are *very* drafty—a sign that gnomes are finding their way in. If you feel a draft or chilly gust, do your best to follow it to its source and try to identify the weak point in your defenses. If you're having trouble doing this yourself, enlist the help of your local power company. Request an "energy audit" and let a professional locate the breach.

Logbook of Strange Phenomena

Keep a logbook on hand to chronicle any and all unusual happenings inside and outside the house. As the frequency of unusual phenomena increases, so does the likelihood of an attack. Details to note include the following:

- ▲ What was the nature of the strange event?
- ▲ Where did you see this unusual occurrence?
- ▲ What was the date?
- ▲ What time of day was it?
- ▲ Were you alone?
- ▲ Were you indoors or outdoors?
- ▲ If indoors, in which room or area of your house did the sighting occur?
- ▲ If outside, was the sun out? Was it raining? Describe the temperature.
- ▲ Have you seen this sign before? Is this a recurring phenomenon?

Although the notations may seem pointless now, if an attack were to commence and you live to tell the tale (and you will—think positive!), such a journal will prove invaluable to researchers. Other gnomeowners will be able to pinpoint a pending attack within days or even hours of the actual event—all thanks to your thorough record keeping.

3

RECOGNIZING COMMUNICATION

Agriglyphs (Mini Crop Circles)

Consider this: Lawn gnomes are positioned all around your property. They sit atop retaining walls, line walkways, skulk beneath hedges and birdbaths, loiter near fountains and other water features, and hang from tree swings. By creating visual cues in the earth itself, a lawn gnome can avoid suspicion—because the communication is nonverbal and inaudible—and signal to a colleague from any distance or angle. They often use these agriglyphs when other options have been compromised.

Agriglyph is a term coined by the late celebrated Scottish agronomist Sir Hamish Tootler-Murphy, who disappeared under suspicious circumstances in a backyard in eastern Connecticut on July 17, 1979. Agriglyph joined the formal gnomenclature in 1977, but evidence that it had already entered the vernacular exists as early as 1974.

So how are agriglyphs created? Like the classic cornstalk crop circles, the mini glyphs are made by bending tall blades of grass in the same direction. Whether this is done by one gnome or many remains unclear. You've probably already seen these designs in your lawn but not thought much of it. Well start thinking of it now. Better yet, start translating. "These are clear signs that lawn gnomes are preparing for an invasion," says garden symbologist Elizabeth Wayfield. "It's like tarot cards. Different symbols mean different things.

Some symbols mean it's time for the homeowner to get the hell out of Dodge."

The first line of defense toward discouraging the insidious mini crop circle is to deprive the perpetrator of his materials; in other words, maintain a regularly and closely mown lawn.

Mazes

Not so much communication as gameplay, a maze on your property should still alert you that something is very wrong. Why? Because the design of the maze is actually a copy *of the floor plan of your home*. This means *they've gotten inside* and they're *practicing how to attack you within your own walls.* However, this explanation has only been verified on three occasions, and mazes are generally thought to be used primarily for gnome recreation and mind-sharpening activities.

Mentions of mazes can be found in some of the earliest writing on human-gnome contact. In her 1969 landmark book, *A History of Mazes and Gnomes*, architectural historian Margaret Olsrant details the uncanny correlation between large estates in Europe that possessed boxwood hedge mazes and topiary labyrinths with gnome ownership.

Sometimes the labyrinths are relatively simple, with rudimentary patterns of stones laid out on a forest floor—or your front lawn (see "Stonescaping" on page 24). The most intricate and exquisite mazes are hedge mazes—sculpted out of brush and thicket—used to sharpen a young gnome's fight-or-flight acumen. If you see a hedge maze on or near your property, you're in trouble for two reasons. First, the gnomes have grown so brash they're not afraid of attracting your attention. Second, complex hedge mazes are usually created by a gnome elder, or "wise man," as an artistic Magnum Gnomus. The fact that a chieftain lives near you is bad, bad news.

Stonescaping

Much like agriglyphs, the art of arranging stones, or stonescaping, to convey intention is another cunning means of nonverbal communication. Stones may be arranged or aligned in straight lines (to indicate the point of entry for the forthcoming attack) or arranged in circles or other patterns. Though unfamiliar to our eyes, such arrangements may also represent words or phrases in Gnomish (and, currently, the human race lacks an accurate lexicon for their language, making translation impossible).

This skill with stones extends to weaponry design. Gnomes will file small rocks and pebbles to a sharp point and use them as ammunition in slingshots. On file with Germany's Federal Criminal Police Office (File No. GN3416) is the recently declassified case of a suburban Berlin gnomeowner who refused to

leave his home for months, fearing a gnome attack. One day, the man noticed water seeping in under the back door, flooding his kitchen. Upon opening the door, he saw that large stones had been positioned to redivert water from a nearby storm drain, creating an aboveground watercourse—all part of a plan to get him to open the door. When he did, he was attacked—mercilessly. Luckily, a neighbor arrived minutes later and found him in a coma. The gnomeowner eventually regained consciousness and made a full recovery. Later he launched an awareness campaign about the hazards of gnomeownership and the consequences of stonescaping.

Lights

Gnomes are known to use light-based communication as a means of "talking without talking" using Gnome Morse Code—an ideal method of transferring nonverbal information. Nocturnal communiqués require handheld lamps or lanterns. No translation for Gnome Morse Code exists at the current time. Assume all messages are lethal.

What is important to take away from this is that gnomes are using homemade heliographs to converse with one another while you're ten feet away digging up radishes you won't even eat anyway. So don't be distracted by *how* they're doing it. Pay attention to *why* they're doing it: 1) Assess and confirm that they *are* communicating, and 2) destroy/confiscate anything that could aid such communication.

To assess and confirm, study the following scenario: You stand close to a gnome on a swing. As you move past the swing (at a normal walking pace), a beam of light hits your eyes. It's

not a direct shot from the sun but rather a reflection from somewhere else—but where? Aha! It came from a mirror ball on the *other* side of the yard. Bingo. Now you know they're communicating. Take note in your journal and, using a long implement (a hockey stick, broom handle, or garden rake), separate the gnome from his light sources. Do not use your hands for this task. You've just bought yourself a few more days.

Would it shock you to know that many English idioms we use today (that you thought were harmless) can trace their origins to man's ongoing war with garden gnomes? **Gnomenclature: Acts of God** is a phrase that first appeared in the fine print of a Censa Insurance contract in 1915. Censa had been sued by a woman in Arkansas who claimed to have lost three fingers in a "garden statue attack" in 1914. Coincidence? We think not. Later, in 1916, Censa added "natural" disasters such as floods, hurricanes, and lightning strikes to their standard policy language.

PROTECT

4

—

PASSIVE FORTIFICATION— AREA DENIAL

Here are the facts: You have lawn gnomes in your backyard, on your block, in your neighborhood.* They're out there, moving around—conspiring to kill. You're stuck between a rock and a hard gnome blade. What are you going to do? You can't, in all good conscience, give them away. You can't just pack up and move (and even if you did, who's to say with absolute certainty a few bearded hitchhikers wouldn't stow away in your U-Haul?).

No no no. What you're going to do is fight back. What is needed here is a multipronged approach to repel invaders and fortify your residence. Your first order of business is a comprehensive program of passive fortification. With traps and barriers, your goal is what military experts call *area denial*. In other words, you want to create a barricade of sorts

* You may be totally screwed.

to stop them from getting near your house. This will be followed by steps for gnomeproofing the exterior of your home (*access denial*) before taking protective measures inside your dwelling (*internal defense*). There's lots to be done, so finish your coffee and get to work.

Trapping for Containment

When it comes to trapping a lawn gnome, the more primitive and basic the ensnarement, the better. First, dig a hole in the ground at least 3 feet deep. (Feel free to make it deeper.) Make sure that the sides are smooth so that when your victim falls in your makeshift oubliette, he cannot climb out. This will be your "cage." If you're feeling extra aggressive, fill the bottom with spikes, stakes, razor wire, or something sticky.

Disguise the hole by liberally covering it with leaves, shrubbery, twigs, and other greenery. The trap is now camouflaged. (Make sure not to step on it yourself! That's an ideal way to break an ankle.) Now you wait, checking the trap frequently but unobtrusively—you don't want to tip off an observant gnome.

When approaching a trap with a gnome inside, your best bet is to immediately fill the trap with cement, encasing the gnome in a most unpleasant death. When the cement has dried thoroughly, you'll be left with a handsome—and permanent—garden statue.

Constructing a Moat

Gnomes can't swim, so water is one of your most reliable allies. Just as medieval castles were protected by large-scale moats to keep attackers at bay, you can surround your home with a similar deterrent.

Simply dig a trench at least 2 feet deep and 4 feet across around your house. (Ask your friends or neighbors to help you—this is no task to tackle on your own.) Then fill with water.

A grown human will be able to cross such a barrier with a wide stride or perhaps a small leap. Lawn gnomes, on the other hand, will be looking across a river-size body of water.

Though lawn gnomes cannot cross a well-constructed moat by swimming, they may try to ford it by other means. Be vigilant; look for evidence that gnomes have crossed or attempted to cross your moat. The most common signs include large mushroom caps (gnomes use them as floatation devices) or parallel sticks and twigs used to fashion a makeshift raft or crude bridge.

Gnomes may be small, but they are smart—they know that twigs break and mushroom caps sink; that's how gnomes are gno more. If you're lucky, they'll ditch their assault plans and leave you alone. But don't count on it. Be alert and keep looking for evidence that they are attempting to cross.

Lastly, beware relying on a moat when the temperature drops. As the top layer of water begins to freeze, it forms a usable ice bridge. Break up the frozen crust on a daily basis to keep your boundary secure, or add a little sodium chloride (NaCl) to lower the water's freezing temperature. But be wary—and carry a pitchfork or an aluminum bat when inspecting your moat.

Mixing Quicksand

Did you know you can make your own quicksand? (Well, if you *did*, you no doubt have already tried concocting some.) Quicksand is simply sand mixed with salt water—in specific proportions and under specific circumstances. In nature, it is often found on riverbanks, so you could set up several quicksand traps on the houseside of your moat. That way, if any lawn gnomes did successfully ford the waterway, they would be in for yet another surprise.*

You can locate your quicksand pit in the middle of your yard, or position it at the base of a large tree. If you choose to use an actual sandbox, make sure your children and neighborhood kids keep their distance.

* In a memoir describing her lifelong battle against garden gnomes, Armenian lawyer Ralda Mamikanyan describes, in detail, how the most satisfying moment of her life was watching a lawn gnome sink into homemade quicksand while struggling desperately to escape, to no avail.

First, dig a wide, shallow pit, no more than 2 to 3 feet deep. For the quicksand, the formula is 1 part cornstarch, $3/4$ part milk, 1 part sand, plus 1 tablespoon of maple syrup per part. Stir this mixture (a broom handle or golf club works well) or a sturdy stick, then add 1 salty part water for each part of the mixture. Sprinkle some dirt, grass cuttings, or leaf litter over the surface so your pit is less suspicious looking.

Although time-consuming, building a sink pit like this can really pay off. If the pit is dug correctly, a gnome will sink—slowly—and perish. All that will be visible is his pointed hat. Such visual evidence is quite an effective deterrent to others who may be planning an attack. Plus, there's a good chance other gnomes could sink while trying to save the first one. Lastly, a row of gnome hats sprouting from your yard makes for an interesting garden display.

5

GNOMEPROOFING YOUR EXTERIOR—ACCESS DENIAL

Ammonium Phosphate Fertilizer (Miracle-Gro)™

What's better than some synthetic lawn fertilizer to make your yard the envy of the neighborhood? A green yard *and dead gnomes*—that's what. Want an explanation? Let's dig deeper.

As you fight for your life against these relentless little lawn trolls, you'll find yourself battling on several fronts. One underrated front is herbicidal warfare. When doused on soil, synthetic fertilizers create an unhealthy mix of zinc, copper, and chlorine. Typically, humans aren't affected because we breathe air at least five or six feet above the ground, and the noxious mixture is safely diluted at this distance. But for those at lawn latitude, the toxicity is ever-present.

Select a known congregation area for dowsing—then stand back and watch gnomes go batty. Keep an eye out for strange behavior, such as gnomes falling down, gnomes eating grass, and gnomes pitching headfirst into water.

As always, use caution when approaching a gnome for disposal. There is data to suggest that a crazy gnome may be more dangerous than a normal one. An insane gnome "under the influence" may decide to self-immolate (set itself on fire) then crash into your bedroom kamikaze style. Granted this is a worst-case scenario, but it has been known to happen.

Motion-Activated Lighting

Motion-activated lights are an effective deterrent against prowlers and are more affordable than you may think. Purchase two 60-watt bulbs to cover the least secure entry points of your home, such as the back door and side entrance. When the lawn warriors come for you, they will come under cover of darkness. They know and you know that illumination levels the playing field: when outdoor motion-activated lights are triggered, the homeowner appears with a weapon. Thus, gnomes associate the protective lighting with a heightened state of owner defense and stay away.

However, it is unwise to rely too heavily on any defensive device. Nothing takes the place of vigilant personal observation. Triggering the motion lights can be a ploy to divert your attention while crafty marauders enter from another door or window. As always, avoid predictably routine behavior.

Unattended Ground Sensors and Tunneling

If you've taken the principle of area denial seriously, gnomes have no choice but to try to tunnel *under* your moat or your house. And once they're inside, you're basically SOL.

Unattended ground sensors will alert you to any tunneling activity under your home. These rugged modules work for months without attention, and give you peace of mind—especially if your house has a sublevel (basement). The last thing you want when you're downstairs playing video games is to glance up and face a hoard of saw-wielding gnomes busting through the wall.

Do keep in mind ground sensors are not cheap, and you'll have to purchase at least four—one for each side of the house. In addition to tunneling gnomes, ground sensors will also pick up burrowing animals, such as groundhogs, prairie dogs, gophers, and moles. It would be a shame to go to Def Con 1 over a crazy chipmunk.

Chimney Caps

A full seal is recommended for all types of chimneys. Yes, I realize you can no longer roast marshmallows with the kids, but that's a small sacrifice considering the alternative. And don't go for a weak (cheap) mesh screen—pay the money and get peace of mind. First, remember to shut the flue, then seal off the chimney completely with an additional metal covering and *bolt it down.*

If gnomes anticipate this move (perhaps you've spoken openly of it for some time), they may try to sabotage your roof, perhaps loosening some shingles so you slip and fall during installation. Keep your eyes peeled for any manipulated surfaces.

A Big %&*! Dog

Perhaps the smartest addition you can make to your household is a great big dog. A large pooch can easily corner and disable a lawn gnome inside the house in close quarters or deflect a broader assault on several fronts outdoors. When choosing a breed, look for imposing appearance—yes, size matters. Consider German Shepherds, Boxers, Giant Schnauzers, and Rottweilers. However, most any sizable mixed breed will staunchly defend its territory.

That said, a crafty gnome could easily trick a trusting pet into drinking, say, tainted water. Gnomes will no doubt try to incapacitate Lassie before making a try for you. So if your dog suffers a sudden illness or seizure, it's a bad, bad sign. Seek immediate veterinary attention—after securing your property.

Alternate Postal Options

Your mailbox is what gnome experts call a "hot spot" and a
high-probability area for a gnome attack. When you reach
into the box, that excruciating pain shooting through your

arm means only one thing: You're screwed. A gnome will use his decided size advantage to impale and immobilize you while the others attack *en masse* from nearby shrubbery. The only completely safe alternative? Get a P.O. box.

Off-site mail collection is not without its perils. Because you'll be leaving your house more frequently to pick up the post, avoid predictable travel times and vary your route. Don't be an easy target!

6

GNOMEPROOFING YOUR INTERIOR— INTERNAL DEFENSE

Trapdoors

There are all kinds of options for trapdoors (or should we say, "trap floors") but, again, remember: *simple is better*. Rather than messing with complex piston-powered moving parts or costly subterranean waterslides that spit the trapped gnomes out miles away, opt for a hole in the floor with a small area rug or floor mat to cover it. The principle is elegantly simple: A garden gnome will enter the house, and as he crosses the floor, will step on the area rug and plunge down into the hole, where he will be trapped until he can be destroyed.

Timely dispatch and disposal is key. Given enough time, a trapped gnome can escape or be rescued by his comrades. In all instances of successful entrapment, avoid a subsequent ambush by thoroughly investigating the room for a hoard waiting to strike.

Tainted Beverages

Crawling under houses, climbing down chimneys, and tunneling through walls and floors is thirsty work. No wonder gnomes are festive drinkers and eaters, consuming no fewer than seven meals per day. So when they do arrive inside your domicile, they will be tempted to look for refreshments.

Leave tainted drinks in a variety of locations and vary the levels of fluid in each cup. A mug that looks a little "too easy" or "perfect" will rightfully draw suspicion from an inquisitive intruder.

There are many chemical options to choose from, but none more effective than the bulb of a red squill. Because of its flavorful scent, it is virtually irresistible to a parched lawn warrior. Though it may require thirty minutes to take effect, red squill is much preferred to other toxins, such as warfarin and coumatetralyl (common mouse poisons), which take up to two weeks to completely incapacitate a victim. An inexpensive alterative is common antifreeze, which will work just as well. However, its distinctive smell could tip off a sensitive gnose, so you'll have to mix it with a pungent-smelling beverage, such as a dark beer, to mask its special ingredient.

Naturally, don't drink anything yourself! And do warn *invited* guests that helping themselves could mean a trip to the emergency room.

Glue and Diatomaceous Earth

The glue stick is an affordable tool used for cornering gnomes. Choose an instant-drying, clear, permanent brand and apply it to a slick flat surface such as vinyl flooring or bathroom tile (so you can scrape it off later). Garden warriors traipsing through the area will quickly find their boots stuck to the kitchen floor. To escape, they will be forced to abandon their foot gear and jump backward, away from more glue—and more important, away from *you*.

I have met several homeowners who swear by diatomaceous earth, though an expert opinion (and supervised research) is still lacking. Diatomaceous earth is a naturally occurring fossil-mineral compound, and serves as a similar weapon to a caltrop or barb on the ground. Although not large enough to harm a shod human, these tiny fragments will pierce the unshod foot of a startled gnome. Sprinkle some of this powder into your carpet. As soon as a gnome loses his shoes in your glue trap, he will have to retreat across what to him will feel like broken glass. (Your watchdog will be free of fleas and ticks to boot!)

I can't stress this enough: A gnome that's stuck to the floor is *not* dead nor is he unconscious; don't forget that he is a whirling dervish of death that you must disable *from a distance* before advancing any closer.

Papier Mâché Dummy

Making a papier mâché dummy head is a great project to do with the kids on a rainy Saturday afternoon. And hey, it worked for three Alcatraz inmates who escaped, so why not follow in their footsteps? It you have multiple bedrooms in your house, rotate where you sleep every night to throw off intruders who have been watching your movements, looking for patterns. Close the blinds and curtains at night to keep them guessing.

In the bed(s) you don't occupy, place worn clothing under the sheets to form what will appear to be a body. On the pillow, place your papier mâché head, turned away from the bedroom door to make it more difficult to identify. With any luck, on the night gnomes make an all-or-nothing onslaught, they'll attack the dummy by mistake, giving the real you precious minutes to either gather arms or hightail it out of there.

Air Vents and Heating Ducts

You've seen the *Mission Impossible* movies where the good guys crawl through the ventilation shafts. Well, that's probably happening right now, all around you, except that it's the bad guys. I know what you're thinking—you've got to seal these openings shut asap! But, alas—this is impractical. You need fresh air circulating around your house, and you'll need heat in the winter, so you can't seal off the ducts completely. What you *can* do is use a strong caulk to lock the vents in place so gnomes can't squeeze through the slats (or retreat if they're already in).

Tackle one vent at a time. Remove the grate—unscrew it from the wall or floor—and place a tube of caulk in a caulking gun. Much like using a hot glue gun, spread a thin line of caulk all around the inner edges of the vent openings to "freeze" the vent. Allow the caulk to set for several minutes, then press the grate back into place, and screw it back into the wall or floor. Granted, it's not a permanent fix, but a caulk-stiffened grate is surprisingly resilient and will effectively block or stall most gnome activity.

This can be a dangerous activity if gnomes are already moving through your ventilation system. A gnome could maul you the second you remove a grate, so exercise all the usual precautions before doing so.

If a gnome is already in your air ducts and gets trapped in there, it will die and you may smell unpleasant odors for several weeks unless you dispose of it quickly. (See page 82 for proper disposal techniques.)

Evaluate Vulnerable Points of Entry

Windows: Naturally, gnomes cannot open a closed window. But what about five lawn gnomes? Eh—it's happened before. Always keep your windows locked (yes, even in the spring and summer months) unless you *wish* to die.

Doorways: A locked, two-door system is a very safe bet against lawn gnomes. But, two major caveats: First, if you have a pet door, you're in trouble. (In fact, a lawn gnome could be

behind you right now! Be careful! Is everything okay? Good. Whew.) Second, lawn gnomes will try and sneak inside during those brief moments when you enter and exit the house. Your best guard against this is to stay alert—*and don't forget to look down.* Install outdoor and motion-activated lighting at all entrances, and always have a look-see before entering or exiting your residence.

Attic: You may have already battled raccoons, mice, squirrels, possums, or bats taking refuge in your attic. If these critters are clever enough to get in, multiply their cleverness by fifty—then add psychopathic tendencies. Maybe *then* you're close to imagining a gnome in your attic. The truth is, an attic is hard to fortify because there are so many odd ways to enter it. So instead of trying to cut off access altogether, set traps for containment. In other words, let the gnomes in. Just don't let them out alive.

Chimney: They come down the chimney, like jolly St. Nick—but deliver evisceration and death. See page 42 for the chimney cap option. If there's a legitimate reason you can't seal the top of your chimney, block up the fireplace using bricks and mortar to seal it from the bottom. Best option? Do both.

Gnomenclature: Baker's dozen is an expression that evolved after a series of strange deaths occurred throughout rural France in 1959. Following an intensive investigation by Interpol, one fascinating common denominator was revealed: villages where garden gnomes were prominently displayed *near the local bakery* were murder-free; villages where gnomes were not displayed near bakeries or patisseries were awash in human blood. The connection? Freshly baked bread. Word spread across the countryside that leaving a warm, fresh loaf outside a bake shop would attract—and pacify—serial killer garden statues. This ploy became so successful, many bakers added an extra loaf for every twelve ordered—a practice that continues to this day.

DEFEND

7

—

TEN TIPS THAT COULD SAVE YOUR LIFE

1. Practice exiting from a first-story window. This is not as straightforward as it may seem. When your house is on fire or garden gnomes are clawing at your legs, simple motor functions such as turning the lock on a window and calmly stepping through it suddenly become unimaginably difficult. So, as with all challenging tasks, you must practice. Get yourself acquainted with unlocking a window, lifting up the sash, kicking out a screen if necessary, then stepping through and exiting as quickly as possible.

The recommended method for exiting is one leg first, then the other. As you bring your second leg out, the momentum will force you to fall the short drop to the ground. Familiarize yourself with the sensations of falling and landing. Also, note how to bend your body (the angle should be no greater than 45 degrees) when exiting through the window. When seconds count and you *must* jump—dive headfirst.

Although you run the risk of a neck injury or concussion upon landing, a feet-first "thread-the-needle" leap through a window takes exceptional agility.

2. Memorize room layouts. Do you know how many stairs connect the first and second floors? How many paces it takes to walk across the dining room? Where to find the deadbolt on your back door in the pitch dark? These are the questions you must answer "yes" to, if you wish to survive. When the power goes out, you've got less than a minute before the first gnome attacks, statistically speaking. Even if they don't cut the power, you could be blinded by flashing lights or eye powder. Take mental notes of the layout of each room, and practice navigating while blindfolded.

Gnomenclature: Fiddling while Rome burns dates back to when a sizable chunk of ancient Rome was destroyed by fire. Legend has it that the emperor Nero sawed away on a fiddle as his imperial capital went up in flames—further worsening his already poor standing with his Roman subjects. But wait. A recently discovered and newly translated eye-witness account tells a different tale. A palace slave by the name of Calpurnius was serving Nero supper when he noticed the "small wooden man-doll" (affectionately named "Fiddle" by the emperor because of the tiny stringed instrument clutched in his carved fist) had fallen face down onto a burning oil lamp, igniting a conflagration. Word spread through the city like, well—like wildfire—and the story changed with each telling, morphing into the version we know today.

3. Keep a weapon in every room. If they strike, you must fight back. Every room needs a weapon—and that weapon should be stored in a place where gnomes cannot easily tamper with it, and always keep it within two steps of you. Mounting an ax or pitchfork on the wall is an aesthetic as well as practical choice.

4. Practice rising from bed in attack mode. The goal is to go from sleeping and vulnerable to combat-ready in less than one second. It will take several nights of practice to achieve this: When awoken in the night you want to pop up quickly and open your eyes wide, letting them adjust to dark or ambient light as quickly as possible. With your left hand reach for a portable illumination source (flashlight), and with your right hand reach for your weapon. While you're at it, practice sitting up quickly while yelling as you do so. Startling movement combined with a loud yelp will spook a stealthy gnome.

5. Keep floors clear. If you must move in the dark, the last thing you need is to trip over your dog's chew toy or give your position away by stepping on Sunday's newspaper. Keep floors clear of all objects, including animals and children. Before you go to bed, examine each room and remove anything that could hinder your flight path. To prevent stepping on sharp items (steak knives, blender blades, and the like) or, God forbid, an actual gnome—never, *ever*, go barefoot and *sleep with your shoes on* so you can hit the ground running.

6. Store flashlights in handy, multiple locations. Gnomes will no doubt cut your power prior to a formal siege. Therefore, you will need a flashlight in every room.* To effectively prepare yourself, unscrew lightbulbs from lamps and overhead fixtures, so that when you rehearse a gnome attack, you can replicate the experience of flicking on a light switch and having nothing happen. Don't be stingy. Buy several heavy-duty flashlights, such as Mag™ lights, that can double as blinding and bludgeoning instruments in addition to illuminating your evacuation.

In addition to flashlights, consider investing in a battery-operated "clapper" (yes, like the ones you've seen on late-night TV commercials). How do they work? Let's say a gnome enters the house and you're awoken by a steak knife dropping on the carpet (and yes, you will soon be so finely tuned to gnome activity that this alone wakes you up). As you sit up and gather your bearings, you clap twice to activate battery-operated lighting. Illumination occurs, and you're already reaching for a weapon and screaming to scare the bejesus out of your intruder. Now *that's* being prepared.

7. Keep countertops clutter-free. Keeping bathroom counter surfaces clear of clutter is another important safety tip. Bathrooms in particular are veritable deathtraps because

---

* If you have a backup emergency generator that will power on floodlights inside and outside your dwelling, then this step is less crucial than the others.

many places exist for a gnome to "hide in plain sight." Think twice—no—three times before reaching blindly for the shampoo. Personal hygiene is important, but is it worth *your life*?

8. Have a second bicycle. Attacking gnomes will likely disable your automobile, so you must have an alternate means of transportation. Gnome expert Thomas Bayley offers this advice: "Studies have shown that homeowners with two or more bicycles have the best survival rate. Will gnomes cut wires and slash tires in your car? Absolutely. Will they slash your bike tires? Possibly—and that's why I recommend keeping a 'dummy' or 'decoy' bike available. The gnomes will see this bike and disable it, but your 'real' ride will be close at hand."

9. Don't yell "Help." Classic advice from law enforcement is to scream "Fire!" rather than "Help!" if you're being assaulted. The reasoning is that bystanders are wary about approaching to give help because they fear for their own safety. And if you're under attack by gnomes, this is a perfectly reasonable concern. Rather than shrieking "Fire!" instead try, "Call the police!" This lets them know *you're not the threat.*

10. Install a panic button. If an attack is in progress, a panicked phone call to the cops is not recommended. For whatever reason, law enforcement personnel have never taken reports of garden gnome attacks seriously. (This is a worldwide problem.) So if calling 911 is not an option, what can you do? Try investing in a panic button. It will cost you a moderate monthly fee to have security and medical personnel on call 24/7—and it's worth it. Here's how it works: As soon as the raid begins, hit the button and a dispatcher will call to verify a problem. If you can't respond, the dispatcher will send assistance immediately.

8

Their Arsenal

Gnomes are more than capable of turning household items, kitchen utensils, and office supplies into lethal weapons that they will use *against you*. What follows is but a small sampling.

Sickle, Scythe

The sickle is the classic weapon of choice for adult lawn gnomes. Handheld with a curved blade, it is ideal for cutting, slashing, and causing victims to defecate themselves upon realizing just how sick a weapon it really is. Although the sickle is the preferred weapon for today's gnome, warriors of olden times were partial to the scythe, which is a longer, shallower blade attached to a long stick, often with a secondary gripping handle. (This is fitting, as the scythe is also the iconic symbol of the Grim Reaper.)

Flashing Lights

This is classic gnome misdirection, plain and simple. You see flashing lights on a wall, ricocheting around a chandelier. You're spellbound, perhaps even hypnotized a little—and that's when the attack comes. Beware of rooms with mirrors. Reflected lights can throw off your equilibrium, dull your reflexes, and weaken your defenses.

Spear

Easy to use, a spear usually starts out as a harmless stick lying around in your backyard. A gnome warrior will collect the stronger, stouter fallen branches and file down an end to form a sharp point. Depending on length-versus-velocity-versus-distance when hurled, a spear is equivalent to the average kitchen knife and will cause moderate to serious injury. Spears are usually thrown (so gnomes can keep a safe distance from their victims), but they are also used like bayonets for close-range, repeated stabbing.

Bow and Arrow

A classic weapon and still dangerous. A gnome arrow tends to be small, and will not inflict much intrinsic damage to its target—and that's why the tips typically are dipped in poison. If you pluck an arrow from your skin, you have approximately 90 minutes to call poison control or get to a doctor before full paralysis sets in.

Axe, Hatchet

Axes are cumbersome and heavy, so it's rare to see an ax-wielding gnome anymore. Even if they manage to land a direct blow, the blade may lodge itself in a bone or limb, making a repeat hit nearly impossible, *and* giving you time to regroup and return the favor. Because hatchets are smaller and lighter, you're much more likely to run into a hatchet-carrying gnome as he runs into *you*.

Slingshot

The slingshot is the weapon of the youngster, the immature gnome who probably snuck into your house without approval from his elders. Although a slingshot sniper is not lethal in itself, you should be wary if novice lawn gnomes are staging unsanctioned skirmishes on your property. It can only mean one thing: your boundaries are not being respected—and that means something far worse is imminent.

Kitchen Utensils

Ever thought about padlocking your utensil drawer? Well think about it now, before a grilling fork or vegetable peeler enters the base of your spine. If a lawn gnome doesn't have a sickle or other weapon at his disposal, he'll use your own gourmet gadgets against you, including the cheese grater, salad tongs, eggbeater, ice pick, pizza cutter, meat mallet, and those small pointy little corncob holders.

Office Supplies

Keep staple guns, scissors, letter openers, thumbtacks, packing tape, even fountain and ballpoint pens, if not locked away in a drawer or cupboard, then at least under close surveillance. Try storing such items in different locations rather than grouped conveniently together. This will make it a little more challenging for gnomes to arm themselves at your expense.

Toxic Powders

If you see a gnome reach into his pocket and grab a handful of dust, it's not dust—it's explosive powder. When cornered, a gnome can blind you with a dazzling detonation and then flee as you flail about for four to six seconds. *Don't rub your eyes!* Rubbing will only worsen the burn. Instead, try rapid blinking to generate tears that will naturally flush out and cleanse your eyes. Of course, if you've memorized the layout of your home, the momentary loss of vision will not prevent you from finding your way out of the room. Priority one is to get outdoors and into open space. Wearing safety goggles may sound a bit extreme, but they're really the best defense against blinding powders.

9

Your Arsenal

Gnomes are pack hunters—where you find one, you will find many. All warfare strategists suggest that if you lack numerical superiority and/or some kind of tactical advantage, the best strategy is simply *not to fight*. If you enter the house only to find yourself besieged by two dozen gnomes, your best option is to escape. Combating a hoard is only advised when no other choices exist—i.e., they stand between you and the room's sole exit. In this situation, you need weapons, but the more extreme the circumstances, the more extreme the measures you'll need to take to save your life. Do whatever—*whatever*—it takes to get out of harm's way and live to fight another day.

Battling a single lawn warrior requires a different strategy than when facing an insane melee. Your choices will also be guided by locale—certain weapons are ideal when squaring off against an indoor attack versus an outdoor ambush.

Shovel, Rake, Pitchfork

Garden implements are excellent tools for combating garden gnomes at close range. When choosing a shovel, avoid the more typical flat-blade variety. Instead, go for the sharp-tipped spade, which will inflict more harm in less time. It's also a sound idea to purchase several reliable snow shovels.* Don't be afraid to go cheap and buy the ones with the big orange scoops. True, they're not real metal, but they're light and broad and cover more area with each swing, plus the plastic is still sturdy enough to stop a small blade or flying arrow.

Metal garden rakes and pitchforks are *essential* equipment for safe gnome disposal, and do double duty as pinning and dispatching tools.

Hockey Stick

Light, with a long reach given a healthy swing, a hockey stick is a solid choice for combat. But don't buy a girl's field hockey stick. Purchase NHL equipment that's at least 70 inches in length and made of either carbon fiber or Kevlar®. These tougher materials will ensure maximum damage upon contact and are strong enough to withstand multiple incidents.

---

* Voted #1 most underrated weapon, according to a survey of U.S. and northern European gnome defense experts.

Baseball Bat

A bat is not your best option, but not a bad one either. A metal bat is ideal, because it won't break or weaken; it's also lighter yet packs a heck of a wallop. If you have the muscle to use it, get a longer bat—aim for 34 inches. Always purchase the real thing; avoid corked bats or wiffle bats for children.

Because a bat is used for striking a baseball in midair, you may be tempted to toss or "pitch" a gnome and try to knock it into your neighbor's yard. Although we can all smile at this idea, it's *never* wise to strike a gnome as it's careening through the air. If you swing and miss, you're screwed. Instead, move away from a pouncing or falling gnome and allow it to hit the floor or ground. The impact could injure or even incapacitate it, leaving you with a high-percentage opportunity for a successful conclusion.

Furniture

Tables, chairs, and mattresses can serve as both offensive and defensive aids if close-quarter insanity ensues. A chair, for example, will not only injure a number of attackers if thrown, it will also provide one to two seconds of confusion—and that's when you run through the pack, absorbing blows along the way. If you find yourself cornered, turn a table on its side or flip a mattress to block projectiles. Gather your wits and look for the safest route to an emergency exit. No matter what happens, you must get out of the room. If you don't, you will die. Destroy anything you need to; it's just stuff—it can be replaced. You can't.

Garden Hose

Extremely worthwhile but somewhat impractical to use indoors, a garden hose is an amazing exterior defensive tool. A garden hose set at a full-pressure blast can deliver quite a punch and knock a gnome clear out of its rabbitskin boots. Although problematic in drought-stricken regions of the country, it's not a bad idea to simply turn on your hose whenever you go outside.* This will save you precious moments in the event of a sneak attack.

Mace, Pepper Spray

Not recommended. Despite the unverified testimony of a few alleged survivors, there is no evidence that commonly used lachrymatory agents such as mace and pepper spray have the least bit effect on garden gnomes. Skip them and go for proven blunt force trauma solutions.

---

* Nearly 95 percent of recorded garden gnome attacks happen indoors. Although the odds of an outdoor skirmish are small, do not take chances.

Sledgehammer

Not recommended. Although this weapon may seem like an obvious choice, consider its drawbacks: It's very heavy (more specifically, it's top-heavy), is awkward to maneuver, and requires a full-torso swing. Though a large mallet can deliver a devastating blow, the average hammer's surface area is only a few inches—leaving little margin for error. Says gnome defense expert Thomas Bayley: "If you swing and miss, you're left open for attack. Tests show it takes a full three seconds, on average, to recycle and deliver another swing. When you're fighting gnomes in close quarters, two seconds to recycle an attack is way too long. You'd be crazy to pick up a weapon like that."

Firearms

Not recommended. Firearms, in general, make poor weapons when combating an advancing armada of gnomes. Yes, the sound will likely deafen them (possibly you, as well).* But guns jam; they need oiling and care; and the average undereducated gunslinger will more likely injure himself than actually score a gnome casualty.

---

* If your intent is to use the loud discharge to frighten gnomes away, you can always fire blanks. If home destruction is not a concern, then go the whole nine yards and purchase a 357 Signature in a Glock 33, regarded by some as the loudest handgun on the market.

However, if you are familiar with handling firearms, a shotgun may be a suitable "last chance" home defense option. Rather than slugs, use buckshot. The spray of pellets will cover a wide area and take out multiple marauders. The obvious downside to such a weapon, besides the destruction of property, is a possible broken shoulder or clavicle due to the powerful kickback.

Landmines

Not recommended. If you're like me, sometimes you daydream about a lawn gnome tiptoeing through your tulip beds only to be blown to Kingdom Come when it treads on an antipersonnel mine you planted three days earlier. Or—kaboom!—a cluster bomb. Oh, what a glorious sight (and sound) that would be. But let's face it, a landmine is not a good idea, indoors or out. For starters, unless it's buried discreetly by someone who knows what the heck he's doing, local gnomes, even dense ones, will know something's up. But the biggest drawback to a victim-triggered explosive device is that it does not discriminate between friend and foe—thus you are just as likely to step on one by accident as your enemy is.

Flamethrower

Not recommended. It looks cool in the movies, but it's impractical, illegal, and very dangerous. If not handled by a professional, a single burst of fire will result in your whole house burning down.

Your Feet

Not recommended except as a last resort. A well-timed, forceful kick will send a garden gnome flying through the air, no doubt pulverizing at least a few limbs. Quick reflexes will be key. Practice what soccer coaches call "pitter patter"—drills that increase foot speed and agility while also contributing to overall conditioning.

Use the instep of your boot (no bare feet, remember!) and kick *through* the gnome itself, as if aiming a soccer ball into a goal. The *wrong* way to use your feet against a gnome is by trying to stomp on him from above. The reason is simple: The gnome will be armed with a sharp-edged weapon pointing upward. When you attempt to squash the gnome underfoot, your shoe and foot will be punctured, sliced, or diced, thereby turning your once-advantageous situation into a life-or-death struggle.

Your Body

Not recommended except as a last resort—and I mean a really last resort. If you're really in a jam, falling on a gnome might kill it, and will certainly stop it. But it also exposes you to injury. This is a last resort that's (obviously) more effective with "weightier" individuals.

Unconventional Options

A deceased or moribund gnome can make an effective projectile. Is this a bit gross and macabre? Yes. But is it also an inspired instance of "repurposing"? Absolutely. The average garden gnome weighs approximately eight pounds and can be easily tossed across a room by a grown man or woman, even a sturdy child. When chucking a gnome in a defensive manner, an underhand pitch is the most practical approach. Throw him as you would a softball. For the more advanced "gnome bowler," a sidearm style, as if skipping a stone across a pond, is another method, affording more precise aim.

Gnomenclature: The grass is always greener on the other side. In a strange display of aesthetic one-upsmanship, garden gnomes have been known to compete with one another when placed in adjacent yards. The objective is to nurture the greenest, most perfectly manicured lawn possible, known colloquially as "the grass is always greener." Garden gnomes have been observed taking extreme, even bizarre measures to enhance their yards, including speaking to individual blades of grass, diverting compost and fertilizer from one property to another, and deliberately disabling neighboring sprinkler and irrigation systems.

Disposal

I would be remiss if I did not cover the basics of dead garden gnome removal. If you've tangled with a gnome inside the house, and you are positive the menace moves no more, your best course of action is to incinerate the little bastard. *Do not bury him in the backyard*—unless he can be completely entombed in poured concrete. Several former gnomeowners, apparently now living in a substrata of the Federal Witness Protection Program, have described a postmortem phenomenon similar to the so-called *Pet Sematary* syndrome. This alarming scenario involves the reanimation of dismembered, but improperly interred lawn statues. Although these reports are unsubstantiated, I and other gnome defense experts and analysts feel it is unwise to discount them.

Locating the appropriate incinerator may not be as easy as it sounds. The $50 garden incinerators you find online can't handle this job. You'll have to contact your local hazardous waste removal service (this is expensive), or locate an industrial incinerator and take the supervisor out for a beer. The goal is to buddy up with the person in charge so you can make periodic "dropoffs" on an as-needed basis.

Another good (but not cheap) backup plan would be to locate a crematorium in your area.

PART
4

APPLY

10

Mortal Combat

If you do everything advised in this book, there is a very, very good chance you will never find yourself in a moonlit room, desperately engaged in hand-to-hand combat with a ravenous hoard of lawn warriors, fighting for your life. That's the good news. The bad news is that no matter how much preparation you take, *nothing is guaranteed.* Sometimes, you just run into a rogue gnome or a pack of aggressive combatants who *will* pick a fight. When that happens, it's game time.

All I can tell you is this: When that day comes, and you must arm yourself with the intent to kill . . . *you shall be ready.* The gnomes have their weapons; you have yours. They've got a strategy; so will you. Their "edge," if you want to call it that, will be sheer numbers. Remember the adage "Where you see one gnome there are many"? Heed those words. You will make up for your numerical disadvantage with preparation, new skills, advanced weaponry, and hefty jolts of adrenaline. Mentally prepare yourself *now*, and as you do, feel free to tie back long hair, please lose the dangly earrings, and for the love of God take off your necktie if you're still wearing one.

Use Terrain to Increase Advantage

Whether you're fighting one gnome or fifty, you have to recognize the natural advantages around you. After all, this is *your* home turf—no one knows it as well as you. For starters, think about *terrain* and how to maximize it to your advantage.

Let's rewind a bit. In the Middle Ages, defensive towers called *barbicans* were constructed around castles. The barbicans contained dark, narrow, twisting stairwells and passageways, so that if enemy troops did manage to break though a castle's outer defenses, once inside they would have to navigate through a confusing, dimly lit maze. The advantage of sheer numbers was useless because the barbicans were too confining to allow the enemy room to maneuver. These "death traps" (as they were known) allowed a smaller defensive force to repel an attack by a much larger army of invaders. If you're still having trouble visualizing a strategy, consider the Battle of Thermopylae (480 BCE). Despite having a numerical advantage of at least a hundred to one, the Persian army was unable to defeat a small battalion of Greek warriors thanks to a narrow pass (the "Hot Gates").*

---

* You're starting to see a pattern concerning locations designed to limit a numerical advantage—and that pattern involves cool-sounding names. Castles had death traps; Greece had the Hot Gates; what do you have? Phil Martinson, a survivor of a gnome attack outside Pittsburgh in 2005, has designed a residential, combat-ready hallway called "The Devil's Front Door." *Now that's* a cool-sounding name.

So how can you alter your house to slow an advancing gnome hoard from an attack *en masse* to a more manageable one-gnome-at-a-time stream, and thereby create an effective force multiplier? Partially blocking doorways is one of your better bets. Gnomes will have to enter in single file, and their impeded view of the room means they probably won't see your exact location. Confused? Imagine you're entering a bedroom and apparently from out of nowhere a shovel comes crashing down, smashing your friend in front to smithereens. Still think you're up for going in next? Nope—and savvier gnomes will realize they lack the advantage and begin a retreat.

If the Unthinkable Happens . . . and It Will

You open your eyes. It's dark. You're being attacked, or your head and body have been immobilized. Panic sets it. You know what this means. They've got you. And you're about to die. But wait! This is *not* the end. Stop praying and start thinking. You know that others have been there—and lived to tell about it.

1. **Stay calm and remember your training.**
2. **Quickly assess your confinement.**
3. **Whatever you do, do it quickly.**
4. **Get the @#*! out of there!**

A Survivor's Account by "Josh" Talcum

". . . The first sign that something was wrong was the *way* the shower curtain was pulled cross the tub. I never leave it like that. I stopped breathing. For a few moments, all I heard was silence. I was listening hard, straining to hear something—anything—out of the ordinary.

"Then the silence was shattered by a chorus of shrill yelps as they attacked me from all sides. Three landed on top of me, four more in front, and another four (at least) behind me; I felt stabbing pains in my feet and legs. Even if I *had* a weapon stowed someplace—a hatchet under the sink or shovel behind the john—I never could have used it. The bathroom is such a tightly confined space—perfect for an ambush! I knew I had to get out of there, but it was hard to think, never mind move. I tried to recall the three steps (or were there more?) from my gnome defense class.

"I managed to toss several gnomes off me as I kicked my way out of the bathroom, but I was barefoot, and they had scattered sharp pebbles on the floor in the hall. As I was trying to remember where I had stashed my baseball bat, all went black. There was that sudden, fateful *bzzt* you hear when the electricity is cut off. I remained as still as I could, frozen in the hallway, trying not even to exhale. I could hear them all around me—sniffing.

"About twenty seconds later, a glowing light seemed to float toward me from the living room, slowly illuminating my location. There was no time to think. With a push off the wall and a summoning of willpower, I dashed the *other way* through the darkness toward the kitchen and saw the faint outline of a windowpane. Throwing my body against the glass, the impact was surprisingly painless. I fell out the window amid a shower of broken shards and splintering wood. Behind me I could already hear the gnomes milling around inside, growling and bellowing the news that I had escaped.

"I remember thinking that I had to reach my car, but then I pictured the slashed tires, shattered headlights, and broken door handles. I knew I was a dead man. I hobbled to the garage and there was my mountain bike, somehow, untouched. It was excruciating to pedal with bloody bare feet, but the alternative was motivation enough to fight through the pain until I reached town.

"I haven't returned home since that night. Josh isn't my real name . . ."

Gnomenclature: Murphy's Law is a concept that comes to us by way of Irishman and early proponent of the gnome defense arts, Darcy Murphy, who lived by the adage: "Whatever a gnome can do to harass a person, he will." Sociologists later adapted the term "Murphy's Law" in the wider sense, meaning that "Whatever can go wrong, will." It is interesting to note that between 1927 and 1996, Murphy never once left his home in County Limerick. He lived to be eighty-seven years old, proving that education and reparation are the keys to a long and gnome-free life.

11

GNOME ROAM NO MORE

As garden gnomes continue to increase their profile through the popular media of film, television, sports, and literature, this insanity known as "the roaming gnome" manifested like an idea out of the darkest circles of Hell. It is characterized by a human being actually *picking up a garden gnome* and taking it to various well-known locations around the world (Buenos Aires, Paris, Poughkeepsie), where it is then photographed and posted on the Internet. *For the love of God,* why? Good question. No reasonable answer exists. You'll have to ask the gnomeowner.

First of all, let's address some of the immediate problems with this, shall we? Gnomes on goddamn trains, cruise ships, and airplanes for starters—*that* problem comes to mind immediately. (Like when rabbits were imported to Australia, a land where they were not native and had no known predators. The unchecked population *exploded* and created an environmental catastrophe that took decades to recover from.) Bringing gnomes to *any* location *where they are not native and have no known enemies* allows them to proliferate in the new locale, thus compounding the current crisis. Plus, the unsuspecting indigenous human populations that adopt imported garden gnomes may not have the training available to them that is needed when handling large numbers of ornamental lawn statuary. It all adds up to bad news.

But hold on a minute. There may be a silver lining to the "roaming gnome" phenomenon after all. Consider the fact that gnomes are extremely challenging to capture, dispatch, and dispose of—until they invade your dwelling. Come to think of it, leaving them halfway around the world doesn't sound like such a bad idea at all. Keep in mind, though, that it's highly irresponsible to simply ditch Bilbo the gnome at the Dorchester in London, where some innocent doorman could end up floating face down in the Thames with his throat cut three days later. No. Leaving a gnome with a new owner who's unaware of the danger is like pulling the trigger yourself. You must leave it where no one can find it—ever. With that in mind, let me suggest several places for you to visit on your next world trip:

▲ **The Laurentian Abyss:** An Atlantic trench off the eastern coast of Canada. This undersea chasm plunges straight down 18,000 feet (3,000 fathoms) to the bottom—quite possibly the lowest place on Earth. Pay to board a fishing vessel; say you're a writer doing a piece on deep-sea species. When passing over the abyss (use a GPS tracker to locate it), dump the little bugger overboard! (Some gnomes are buoyant, so you will need to weight each individual to ensure he reaches his "final destination.")

▲ **God's Window:** This site features jaw-dropping cliffs located on the border between South Africa and Mozambique. It's primeval forest—the Garden of Eden in the middle of nowhere. Even if a lawn gnome did survive the ridiculous fall down the cliff face (which he probably won't), it would be very hard to navigate such difficult and dense terrain.

▲ **Devil's Rock:** An escarpment (otherwise known as an "insane cliff") outside of Haileybury, Ontario, Canada. The drop is a breathtaking sixty stories

down. The location gets its name from sacrifices made by early indigenous peoples. Perhaps you yourself could make a (gnome) sacrifice and keep the tradition going.

▲ **Ridge A, Antarctica:** Located in a desolate part of the world's most desolate continent, this ridge was recently named by scientists as the world's coldest location. The average temperature in winter is –94°F (–70°C). Since no human has ever actually set foot on Ridge A, settle for getting your diminutive pal anywhere *near* the ridge—and by that, I mean within 500 miles. It will still be remote enough. Hopefully you'll pass on peacefully in your bed long before he's found or manages to reach a research station.

▲ **Manchac Swamp:** A swamp in Louisiana you would
never want to visit unless trying to "disappear" a
gnome. It's said about Manchac, which is not far
from New Orleans, that anything or anyone who falls
into its waters will never be seen again. That's good
enough for me.

▲ **Doorway to Hell:** Also called the "Gateway to Hell,"
this gigantic fiery pit in Uzbekistan seems like something out of a bad movie. Decades ago, geologists
began excavating the area, looking for natural gas
deposits. Not only did they find the gas, but they also
found a seemingly infinite amount of it, leaking from
an underground cavern. Fires were set at the site
to burn off poisonous fumes, and the fires still burn
today. Plunk your pal into the lava-hot crater and
he's as good as gone.

▲ **Cocoa Beach:** A less practical option financially, but a surefire way to rid yourself of gnomes forever is to place them aboard a space shuttle. The last attempt at this was in 2007, when billionaire Felix Emry struck a deal with NASA and spent an obscene amount of money to send "some of his belongings into space." Interestingly, the launch was scrubbed at the last minute due to mechanical problems. But when NASA personnel examined Emry's belongings onboard the shuttle, all they found were "six gnomes of the garden variety." Upon hearing that the launch had been canceled and his possessions were already in the mail headed back to him, Emry ended his life with a pistol. The whereabouts of his "possessions" remains unknown.

Retake the Garden

If you've made it this far, congratulations. You're well on your way to becoming a gnome-slaying warrior who refuses to submit to the "new world order" of sadistic backyard ornaments. You now know how to assess, how to protect, how to defend, and how to drop a gnome off the side of the Earth and watch it disappear into oblivion forever.

You can do it—you're ready.

Let me leave you with the story of British bricklayer Colin Gravelle. Upon seeing the announcement online that a book would soon be released regarding garden gnome attacks, he used up all his calling cards to ring the publishers in the San Francisco Bay Area. His voice cracking, Colin recounted stories of sleepless nights and unprovoked attacks occurring month after month after month. All he wanted, Colin explained, was to have the tools and knowledge necessary to protect himself and his home. In short, he begged for an advance copy of this book. Needless to say, my editor (I can't use her real name) sent one off to Lincolnshire that very afternoon. Time passed, and we all kind of forgot about Colin until a gift basket showed up at the publishing house with a note attached. The note read:

```
To everyone involved in the making of
the gnome book:


    I never thought I would be able to
breathe easy again or even step into my
backyard one more time. I was living
like a hermit, paralyzed by fear. But I
received your book in the mail. Thank
yous (sic). And I took the advice on its
pages. I caught and destroyed six lawn
gnomes in three days. I knew there had
to be more gathering for an assault. But
```

the rest had the good sense to move on. And would you believe I'm writing this letter from my gnome-free backyard? You have saved my life, and for that I am eternally grateful. I only hope others can be saved as well.

Sincerely,
Colin Gravelle

To Colin, our reply is: It was our pleasure. And if they ever come back, take a cricket bat to those little mofos like it ain't no thang.

Postscript

Why do garden gnomes want to kill you? Some experts say it's to gain dominion over your dwelling. Others theorize it's a desire for unlimited access to your goods and possessions. But the truth is: **They're just plan psychotic**. What can you do about it? Assess. Protect. Defend. Apply. Make your home impenetrable and arm yourself to the teeth. Have a plan for the worst-case scenario and don't be subtle about it. As unbelievable as it sounds, a gnome's most reliable ally is, in fact, *you*. That's right—*people just like you* who love garden gnomes and enhance their homes and properties with large collections of lawn statuary. In fact, the number of well-funded organizations *in defense* of lawn gnomes is on the rise, including:

▲ The Gnome Protection League
▲ The Gnome Liberation Army (a.k.a. the GLA)
▲ The International Lawn and Garden Gnome Club
▲ The International Association for the Preservation of Decorative Garden Statues
▲ Foundation for Outdoor Ornamental Figures (FOOF)

Let it be heard loud and clear: If you or anyone in your immediate family is a member of these institutions—*you need help!* If you seek to "liberate" or "emancipate" garden gnomes—you haven't been reading carefully—please reread this book and seek professional help immediately. The only good gnome is a dead gnome. Period.

THE END ... or is it?

ACKNOWLEDGMENTS

The first person to thank is my wife, Bre, for all her love and support. It's not in my nature to throw a story or manuscript in the trash, but if I ever do, she's the type of person who would pull it back out and sing its praises. The second person to thank is my agent, Sorche Fairbank, who believed in this project from the very beginning. And the third person to thank is my editor, Veronica Randall, for loving this book and making it better. These three women deserve more credit than I have page space for.

A big thank-you to Bill Larkin of Indiana, who provided most of the garden gnomes you see in these pages. Others who donated or painted gnomes include Sharon Goss, Donna Briggs, Katie Rigney, Kelsey Murphy, Stephanie Gruenwald, Cori Radford, Julie Bennett, Hayley Gonnason, Lisa Regul, Kathryn Wetzler, and Peter Spreenberg. Also donating gnomes was Plum St. Productions, LLC (plumstproductions.com).

Heartfelt thanks to Betsy Stromberg for the design, Andrew Parsons for the photography, Winifred Yen and Philip Wood for the use of their glorious garden, and Victoria Randall and David Kazanjian for the use of their glorious bathroom. Dogs Calvin and Pancho, you rock! To the human models (who must remain anonymous for security reasons), thank you—you are brave souls.

Lastly, I thank my wonderful family and relatives, as well as Tom and Brian, two good friends who listen to my stupid ideas day after day and have somehow not killed themselves yet. To them, and everyone I forgot, I say *thank you*.